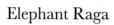

Elephant Raga

# Also by Prartho Sereno

POETRY

*Call from Paris*
*Causing a Stir: The Secret Lives & Loves of Kitchen Utensils*
*Garden Sutra* (a chapbook)

ESSAYS

*Everyday Miracles: An A to Z Guide to the Simple Wonders of Life*

EDITOR/COMPILER

*Everyday Osho: 365 Daily Meditations for the Here & Now*

# Elephant Raga

*poems*

## PRARTHO SERENO

LYNX HOUSE PRESS
Spokane, Washington

*Cover Art by* Grazyna Nowottka: *Elephant on a Parachute in a Parachute,* print on deckle-edged paper,
   8 x 12" This and other art prints by Grazyna Nowottka can be viewed online at *etsy.com/shop/
   emporiumshop.*

*Author Photo:* Angelina Sereno.

*Book Design:* Christine Holbert.

FIRST EDITION

Cataloging-in-Publication Data is available from the Library of Congress.

ISBN 978-0-89924-140-1

# Table of Contents

## ONE

# TWO

# THREE

*for my grandchildren*
Jazzie & Ben
Mr. Q & Mr. N

# ONE

*For our heart still overreaches us,*
*just as theirs did them.*

—Rainer Maria Rilke
*Duino Elegies,* The Second Elegy

# Deplaning

Even at rest the herd flowed in perpetual motion,
the ears like delicate great petals, the ripple
of the mud-caked flanks, the coiling trunks—
a dream rhythm, a rhythm of wind and trees.

*—Peter Matthissen*

At the far end of baggage claim
in pastel shirts and navy blue blazers
they look so longingly in my direction,
jiggling their hopeful block-letter signs—
Hernandez, Patel, Moore—I want to go
to one and say, Yes, I am Mrs. Moore,
then turn and walk with him into a new life.
Yes, I want to say. To everything.
Hyatt Regency, poolside? Yes,
praise the Lord. Oh, thank you—
these bags seem to put on pounds
with each new time zone . . . Am I
attending the conference? Why, yes.
Giving the keynote on my life's work
with elephants. Yes, amazing,
what they have to say—
in registers beneath the human ear.
Expressions of love for which we have
no name. No, I never made out the actual
words, but they taught me with subterranean
patience. I learned to sleep standing
on the savanna, rocked in a long slow
chorus of grass-scented breath . . . Yes,

I see the traffic's terrible this way.
I don't mind at all if you take the back
road. And do tell me about your summer
with the bears. Especially the scrappy one
with the torn-up ear. He led you upriver
to watch the salmon spawn? And you
ate with him. And that fish still flaps
in the pit of you? The fish you shared
with the gleaming, slobbering dark?

# The Hypnotist

Gaze into the spiral as it spins
and you're his. He says you're
a racehorse and your nostrils flare.
He says you're a field of grass and
you sway. He tells you you're an oak
and your legs grow strong, your fingers
twist and tingle toward the light.
You're a rock, and you sink,
a cloud and you untangle, a beggar
with a hidden jewel—warm at last.
But when he declares you lost at sea,
his voice dies to a murmur, and
the snap of his fingers to call you back
is drowned out by the gulls.

# Mirage

*[fr. L mirari—to wonder, more at mirror]*

None but the Aztec King was allowed
a glance into the polished obsidian,
to look in on the otherworld
where the feather-festooned man
swam in and out of the smoke.
Only the Chinese Empress could gaze
down that long silvery hallway
into the future behind her.
The concubines in other rooms were
forbidden, but snatched glimpses
of apparitions in their water bowls—
kohl-eyed and blurry.
It goes on: under the nightfall
of heavy curtains, a girl steals
into her grandmother's room, hovers
over the Russian village of the dresser,
its cobalt-colored bottles and onion-dome jars.
She peers into the blue-black skate pond
of the hand-mirror. But what she sees is nobody
she'll ever come to know.

# The Mother of Ten Thousand Things

My mother meant to yarn her way through—
a regular comedienne. But whenever
she leaned toward the mic, it bloomed.
When she opened her mouth—honey bees!
Handkerchiefs turned to armadillos
in her pockets. And wherever she sat,
the chair would rise, sail her out the door.
Instead of laughter, my mother spread hush.
Instead of shadow, she cast awe.
Bereft of gravity's happy end, she resolved
to redirect the flow, set up coils
on both sides of the bed, a lightning rod
out in the yard. It works, she told me. She didn't
fly so far and away; her feet landed more squarely
in her slippers. She tried to show me and shuffled
over to the beveled window, but her grip
on the monotonous gave way. The prism-edge
broke her into a shoal of minnows
that flashed through the house all day.

# My Chinese Doctor Says

Our lungs billow with grief.
Our livers lug anger, our kidneys
slosh with fear. The heart, she says,
flutters with occasional delight.
She can't remember for a moment
what the spleen is charged with, but
my grandmother had hers lifted out at 93—
so full of something they had to be careful
not to spill it. I imagine that steamy bowl
suspended over the dark continent
of her body, seeping vapors
of talcum and tobacco. Stylish man
in the smoke: fedora and pinstripes.
Hips askew, handlebar moustache,
one eyebrow raised. In a wink
he grows white and senile. Forgets
her name, finds her stew too peppered,
her face too long. Keeps asking after
that other one with skin like a flower,
laughter of a bird. Now my grandmother
is crying in the kitchen, but there are
no winds in these ethers. The spleen
is witness, the doctor remembers—
aloof as it gathers the days into
its bag—oblivious to happiness's
tiny smolder, the rock crags
of anger and spill-offs of fear.
The folded white wings of our grief.

# Temple of Bees

After my friend Baulo drowned,
she lived to tell about it.
*It's just like they say,*
she told me. *Your life flashes*
*before you. But it's not*
*what you think.*

No tambourine chorus
of Bollywood dancers.
No elephants in turbans
or burst of butterflies
from a painted box.

No, what buzzes
through your body
are a billion worker bees,
preparing to swarm off
with their Silent Queen:

stopping at a fire hydrant
to tie a shoe; in line
outside the movie house
as the snow lets go;
mincing onions at the stove,
splatter of rain against
the glass. And your father
looking up at dinner,
asking you to pass the peas.

# Noble Thief

His ultimate virtue
patience,
the angel of stillness
waits
and watches.
It's no good
ripping off a bicycle
or backpack
when a life is puttering along—
well-oiled, cheerful.
He waits till rust
has worn through
the hinges
and your sweater
has lost another button.
Till the faucets
are leaking
and your sweetheart
doesn't call.
He waits
till winter's white tigers
have gnawed
through their cages.
Till they're hungry.
His is not to snatch
the rug out from under;
he wants the floor gone too.
Or better still,
to roll away
the shiny blue ball
on which we spin.

# My Last Blind Date

Sharing his umbrella on our way
back to the BART station,
I was telling him about my stint
with Channel 5 News, how
the cameraman and I drove
to the Projects last summer
after a toddler had fallen
from the fourth story window.
I realize now I shouldn't have
gone into detail—the crumpled
body of the mother who'd
been working at Target while
the teenage babysitter danced
in the next room with the music
bumped up. I should have stopped
before I reached the autumn lake
of her face and migrating birds
in her eyes. The barely audible
cataract of sobs as she rocked
inside her own arms. I knew I'd
said too much when he tugged
my sleeve to blurt: *Careful. You're
headed straight for that puddle*
and when we got to the tunnel
he exhaled goodnight, then broke
into an awkward jog, dodging
the rivulets, leaving me to rock
with her—a jumbled galaxy
in the throes of gathering itself
around a dark unimaginable pull.

# Inheritance

My father
was more
plant
than animal
more tree
a rooted thing
yearning
upwards
his head
a clatter
of leaves
all his life
the light
sifted
through him
to land
at my feet
in perfect
circles
like coins

# In the Hood

*for Jomaine*

You boys from the South Side, deep
in your hooded shirts, suspended
from school till you drop, forever
flash through my memory
on your one-speed Schwinns, standing high
on the pedals. Purple Nikes, flocks
of cellophane and gum wrappers
flaring behind you.

You learned the gamble early:
sing your way free; climb
up the charts. In that upside down
world it's the poets who get to live
above ground—gold chains
and gold-toothed grills, beautiful
rageful eyes. The rest, one way
or another, get disappeared.

And so, dim angel, chattering
in your amber bones, you start
to pray to the street-corner god
who can turn a dime when
nobody's looking.

And burrow deeper into the hood
the lost continent of your face.
When at last a door opens,

it's to an empty cell,
where you rap your vespers—
inadvertent monk
in the solitary confinement
of your song.

# What the Dark Does

The word shimmer
did not originate
with light.
It was brought over
from the blackbirds
as they quivered up
from the fields. They
themselves stole it
from the shadows
of wind-struck trees.
Shimmer leaked up
from the underworld—
coalmines and limestone
caves. Up from hidden fault
and shatter, the quake
of breakage and baritone
rattles in the hills.
Shimmer is what the dark
does when light
saunters up, all brightness
and warmth.
Shimmer is the ragged
breath dark takes
when light draws near.

# Theories of an Alternate Universe

What if your father stuck with ukulele
and harmonica, never went on to circuitry
or became an engineer? Never got
a dependable job that wore him thin
as lightbulb glass. Never lost his mind.

And what if your mom sat so still with her
fears they flew away—a freewheeling
muster of terns that brought her to the shore?
She might have bought a bakery, raised you
on scones and the far-flung songs of sailors.

Or what if you'd decided against the farm,
and your firstborn, Drisana, never gossiped
with the *pillar-cats;* never dragged her feet
through mud till it swallowed her shoes?

It could have been your turn to pick the name,
and instead of breezing through on a psalm, your
second-born, Angelina, would've slogged along
as Rain—a flooded woman with river-rock eyes.

Or you might have stayed in the yard that night
when the clock struck 12, meaning you'd have never
seen them in each other's arms. They might have
carried their secret further down the road, and you
your cooling marriage till you died of hypothermia.

Your tutors might have been cinnamon and terns,
might have been the sea. You might have learned
to give when you met the rocks—fly up and spill over
like breaking waves. Everyone would know when
you were coming: you and your thundering halleluiahs.

# Undertow

The great whales, they say, once cavorted on land—
their closest cousin, the dairy cow. But these
homesick bovines waddled back to the sea,
foreleg morphing to fin, hind leg to fluke.

And so this is the story of a sea creature, wrapped
in her own warmth, and how her heart grew
to the size of a small cathedral, so that when she sang
the notes became round and traveled in rings.

But first, this is the story of a cow, heavy
with barley and wheat, fed-up with gravity
and heat. About the call she barely heard
in the murmur of the sea, and how

her wobbly legs seemed to carry her
on their own, gingering down
over boulder and shale to the shore.

For a few glory days, she cooled her hooves
in the shallows and nibbled on seaweed, but the call
insisted from deeper down and away. So that one day
she strode into the breakers, great head lifted up,

huge nostrils drinking in air. And then
the ocean floor fell out and she drifted down
in a slow-motion paddle, buoyed by something
strange yet familiar—thick, echoing, tasting of salt.

# Ambient Light
## *an Alzheimer's poem*

One day the checkbook felt odd
in his hand. Weightless and foreign-
smelling. New, somehow, in a dog-eared,
tattered way. He was at the rolltop desk
with all its marvelous little compartments,
filled, suddenly, with rare finds
that could be twirled between thumb
and forefinger, held up to the light.

He looked down at the invoice and began
to copy the shapes onto the check:
A . . .  T . . .  T . . .  But the numbers
began to somersault and shimmer. And
by the time he'd gotten back to the check
they'd wriggled off, taking every scrap
of sense along. And so he sat there,
a puddle of sunlight in the cup of his hands.

It went on like this through the days
and weeks, the world growing more
and more slippery, more and more alive.
The hours came close and pressed their faces
into his. The world went wild with its newness,
crooning and carrying on into the night.
And his life came down to a search
for a place to sit and watch the house breathe,
a place from which he could gaze through
the small clean window on the far wall—
so clean these days, it almost wasn't there.

# Mr. James's Marvelous Thing

In this week's obituaries—Betty James,
whose 90 years are boiled down
to three paragraphs, one and a half given
to her husband Richard, the marine engineer
who fell in love with a torsion spring
when it toppled from his desk and
cartwheeled out the door.

In the picture, Betty's holding the beloved
Slinky in her stair-step hands. Most likely
she's been shuffling the toy—one of its many
irresistible charms. But for the picture's sake
she's struck a pose and it has slunk
the way of all things (we were later
to discover)—building up on one hand
before helplessly spilling over to the other.

Her part in the tale was holding it
together—the six offspring and the shiny
empire built around a creature that couldn't rise
to a single occasion but was splendid at descent,
which was what they said about Mr. James,
or at least that's the story Betty stuck to
till the end—that he slunk away,
down to Bolivia to join a cult.

In any case, it was only fair that Betty
share her obituary with Richard, since
it was Mr. James, after all, who gave us

the marvelous thing, and there was little
note taken of *his* passing (somewhere
in the Bolivian mountains, 1974).
And, truth be told, there is never a record
of what the voice says when it calls us
away from the tinseled world, which
leaves us to consider that maybe Mr. James's
tumble south was not so much a fall as a
surrender, a call and response: to rise.

# The Three of Us

In the courtyard of the stone cottage
with its great door and moss-etched
walls, on the Spanish isle of Ibiza,
the three of us—you, Angelina, barely 8;
you, Drisana, a sad-eyed 11; and me,
your thirty-something single mom
with henna-dyed-hair. The duffle bags
are piled up, full of dust and holes.
We dragged them through the streets
of London, in and out of airports,
up and down ferry ramps, over gravel
to our cobblestone *casita*. It's our first
morning—breakfast outside
on overturned buckets, upside-down
crate for a table, chickens pecking around
our toes. You've just bounced back from
the corner store where you'd gone for butter
and milk. You speak Spanish now, you say.
You told everyone, *Aloha*, and they smiled.
And you've figured out the money—how much
peaches cost and the layered pastries you will
convince me to send you back for later. But
right now the sunlight is doing what it loves
best—resting on your uncombed hair.
We're laughing together, rocking on our buckets
under the olive trees, and the birds are laughing along.
Nothing dares come between us—the jets overhead
turn off their engines, the breezes turn back before
they reach us. The surf holds its pose—a curl
of blue-green glass. And the clattering
clockworks of our hearts fall inexplicably still.

# Electrodomestico

One day the iceman came no more.
Neither did the coalman with his telescopic chute.
Nor the junkman with his horse and cart,
his dust and sweat-streaked face.
Not even the milkman's xylophone
of bottles could be heard jangling
through the magenta streets of dawn.

That day the wide-eyed band of women
in calico aprons, pockets bulging with
clothespins, were swept away to a buzzing
world where everything came with its own
complication of cord. But they knew
what to do: take refuge in Houdini's secret
and hide a small brass key in their mouths.

Then they did what they'd always done,
took them all in—the plug-in refrigerator
and washing machine, a menagerie of electric
can openers, ice-crushers, and coffee mills.
And the Edsel of home appliances:
the sit-down steam press that could snatch
a shirt from your hands, send it back
an origami waffle with melted buttons.

It was Fat Tuesday in the history of man's
imagination, a festival of dazzling inventions,
each one out-doing the next. The bobby pin
bowed to the Spoolie, the Spoolie

to the electric roller. The wood-sided
station wagon sidled up, with a radio
and its very own garage.

And the suburbs—that great yawn of grass
with its pastel stutter of houses, stocked
with friendly products: Hamburger Helper
and Bon Ami. A peanut butter named Skippy
and the Quaker smiling with his spoonful of oats.
Here, we were delivered—we girls who grew
into flowers, ceding ourselves to the wind.

And the women watched, incredulous,
as we pulled up those roots, headed out
for the likes of India or Back to the Land.
They couldn't understand why we left
behind our humming dowries—plug-in
frying pans and carving knives, electric brooms.

But on our way out they drew near,
as mothers do, and slipped us the keys—
the small brass keys they'd kept all the while,
in their mouths, but never used.

# Monsoon

Your mother shows up in the grocery-aisle
dream and you tell her she doesn't belong there,
but you can't stop her from wheeling right up
to you: Cheerios tower, empty cart, frizzle
of florescent lights. She meets you head-on.
*Your father is dying,* she says.
Which cues the supermarket storm clouds
to break and rain all over the linoleum floor.
You're dumbfounded, how quickly
everything is swamped—water
streaming from her hair and drenched-through
cardigan, the slosh and squish as you shift
your weight. And in a finishing touch,
the piped-in monotone river of music
floods its banks.

# House on Fire

My house is on fire, but I'm not the man who
stood outside, rapturous in the glow of loss.

I'm inside, passing through fire curtains, the way
we'd pass fingers through candle flames at dinner.

I'm trying to make out the shapes in the smoke:
Uncle Joe with his fighter's nose? And Millie, I think—

his wife, who couldn't stop fidgeting. My father
at the far end, gazing into the chair where nobody sits.

My mother's sad oversized hands. Even the lake
is burning—the cottage my father built from scraps:

maroon and turquoise floorboards, sinks worn-
through to their black iron cores. I dive headlong

into the hottest flames eating the front room away—
us kids strewn on the carpet, consumed in a rainy-day

canasta, whacking at mosquitoes with rolled-up
comics. None of us are saving jacks or nines;

we know half of them are missing.
We're on the lookout for the one-eyed king.

# Disarray

When the tumor in his brain
branched out and gobbled up
reason, my father shot photo
after photo of his workbench
in chaotic bloom. Nothing on its
hook or in its box, all of it heaped up,
an altar to the possible and useless:
old picture tubes and vacuum parts,
screwdrivers, saws, and spilt jars
of nails. Paintbrushes with hardened
hair, striking colorful poses.
O the sublime hullabaloo,
the exploding star. *Let it rip,*
it cries from its hopelessly
disheveled roof.

# TWO

*In the jungle, during one night in each month, the moths did not come to the lanterns; through the black reaches of the outer night, so it was said, they flew toward the full moon.*

—Peter Matthiessen, *At Play in the Fields of the Lord*

# Stories that Need Bodies

**i.**    The girls and I loved Peter Pan—
any story that needed bodies,
so we could dance, lift
our arms, dream ourselves
aloft. Swoop from imaginary gables,
strike an extravagant midair pose.
We would never grow up never
grow up never grow up
my daughters and I.

**ii.**    Dusk dissolves
into the amber hum
of bug lamp,
swish-swash of rocker.

I close one eye
and the world gets bluer.
I close the other and
the porch light comes on.

Moths rise and tumble—
the inimitable cadence
of the flyaway heart.

**iii.**    And now, in the fullness
of night
the black ibis
steals you in her beak,
the dark ark of her wings.

High above a tangle
of strangers,
she opens her mouth.

# Christmas Eve at Rite Aid

Revved up on cocoa and scones,
the nine-year-old twins and I are cruising
the shrink-wrapped aisles.
It's late and this is the only store open
for miles—rattling with lost souls,
gift lists tattered as prayer flags. Names
of the Forgotten leap from every mouth:
somebody's Uncle Pete, Grandma Sal's
new boyfriend, the unexpected guest
whose name nobody can pronounce.

Every one of us is fervent as we burn
our way through the snake-oiled alleys,
past headache tablets and foot creams,
band-aids and lice treatment, itch powder,
baldness remedies, toothache gel.

But the boys know what they're
looking for. Homing pigeons, they light
on aisle B: land of tempera paints, crayons
and flair-tipped pens. Swirled pads
of rainbow post-its. Drunken pirates,
we shovel it in till our baskets slosh
with color. Overcome as I am by the sad
recent news from our astronomers
(the universe is beige—beige as dried grass
and classroom walls), I take my cue
from the young and buoyant on what
to bring the wounded, the thirsty.

# Which Side Are We On?

Ever since the flock of floaters
broke loose in my eye, I can't tell
whether these birds darted down
from the eaves or up
from the snowcaps of my knees.

Same with the ears: Which crickets
are these? Chirping in the limbs
of which trees? What lonesome beast
lows me to sleep? What sea breaks
on which broken shore?

My optometrist says it all comes in
upside-down with a hole in the middle
anyway—a fracas of unsorted data
speeds through, a bewildering
cargo of color and light.

He's trying to console me, but I know
the walls are coming down. The looters
are in, setting off motion detectors,
trip-lights, alarms. Holed up inside
I keep watch for intruders, but who,
at this late date, can tell us from them?

# Elements

## *Birds*

> The mourning dove
> isn't grieving, not
> with this vibrato.
> Even if his love did
> vanish overnight,
> he doesn't believe
> she's gone.

> •

> I saw through us that September
> down to the glass bones,
> mouth-blown cages for songbirds—
> a cacophony of feather dust,
> impossible quivering hearts.

## *Plant Life*

> When you were with me
> the bamboo shadows
> were elegant dancers.
> But I see now
> they are tears.

> •

> All the long
> Mexican *tarde*,

wind, that blustery
*hombre*, fox-trots
his coquette Light
in and out of the pines

•

Five below, snowlight
on the walls, potted tulips
with scuffled heads.
Wind-swept in a world
where you're the only wind.

## Children

On our field trip to the oyster farm
the boys scrambled over the pilings,
tempting the sea. But the girls lingered
in the shelling house, beside the apronned
mammas with pockets full of pearls.

•

Grandson, how
is this polite little world
going to bear you—

thin brown arms stretched
to the ends
as you run full-speed
to meet her?

·

Naked on the sunlit sandpile.
       Is anything
              not a poem?

## Old People

At the sidewalk café, your old friend's eyes
keep puddling up—one whelm after another.
She laughs and says, *That's how it is these days.*

·

3 a.m., I float
past the green
and amber lights:
digital clock,
answering machine,
DVD, VCR.
The runway's lit
and blinking,
but I don't
touch down.

·

By the end, my grandmother
was whittled back to a schoolgirl—in love
with the strapping young nurse. Whenever
someone told her she was 90, she'd laugh
and say, *Who told you that?*

*Color*

In 603, when Prince Shotoku of Japan
forbade the common people color,
women huddled under oil lamps at night,
stitching silk inside their kimonos—
squares of turquoise, red and gold.

# Vespers

Swallow me
Start me again
from your dark-matter
rhapsody

Float me upriver
my celestial tugboat
my phantom barge
sail me home

where cough and ache
and arthritic knee
dissolve back to cloud-breath,
spider-silk, dew

You who gathered me up
undo me: give back my hair
to the cornfields, my toenails
to the beetles,
my skin to the pond

Uncoil the aria
caught in my throat
Return it
to the tongue-tied
sparrow

# Nocturne

Love walks into the kitchen
and turns on the light.
The sound of running water
washes the room.
She is quiet and less picky
than we imagined, happy
at the sink, beside a stack of dishes.
More than anything,
she likes to rinse things
and set them out to dry.

# Discipline

The proprietor of Thai Dreams
Guesthouse is both tuk-tuk
driver and water-taxi walla.
Curb-sweep, porter, vendor
of postcards and all things
teak. A master.

I bring him my demons
of hurry and want, he
gives me time. He bathes
me in it and serves it in tall
cool drinks. For every itch
and ill he offers time. To every
question, his answer is time.

And in his off-hours, he practices—
leans into the coconut palms
or squats at the edge
of the jade-colored sea.
The breezes come
and ruffle his shirt.

# Two Kinds

There are two kinds of people in the world:
the ones with washers and dryers and the ones
who unfurl their slips at the laundromat, spread
saris and bed sheets by the river, hang
their checkered boxers on the line.

There are two: those who love Einstein
for his relativity and those who love his hair.
Those who relish words like *infrastructure*
and *problematic,* and those who like to ponder
life in the belly of a whale. For some,
invitations come as night birds; others get
a summons in the mail. These wander wet and
lonely; those soft-shoe in rhythm with the rain.

Two kinds: the tragic heroes and the understudies;
the bootleggers and the cobblers. Wolf-whisperers
and dogcatchers; shovellers of snow and readers
of the flake. There are the ones who run into the room
with a lit match, stopping to wonder what they came for,
and the ones who run in without the match.

# Scrying with Embers

Late-blooming poppy, top-heavy
and orange on a spaghetti-strap

stem. And tulips—bottomless
undrinkable cups of light.

A coat hook, a shoelace, the grayness
of afternoon gathering into drops

along the eaves. A train station, a basket.
A woman hurrying off to a village

with coffee shops and shade trees,
cooling and edged in ash.

At the glassblower's hut you'll watch
her lift her pipe, breathe a riddle

into the molten jar—a problem that
won't be solved till you drop the glass.

# Signs

*Kamala Beach is one of Phuket's prettiest,*
*but it took a severe beating during the Boxing Day Tsunami.*

*—Lonely Planet Guide, Thailand*

The signs are everywhere.
When the earth moves, they say,
head for higher ground.
Every few meters, like cave drawings:
The wave-shaped blue dragon
and the little stick-people barely
escaping its jaws, running uphill.
One hand points the way, the other hand
offers itself downhill.

Some of the locals talk about it—
tripping as they ran, a stranger's
hand pulling them out.
Saving their lives.
*But not father's*, she quickly adds.
*He too old for run fast or far.*

She shows you photos of the aftermath, kept
from salt and sand in a plastic sleeve—
everything reduced to a smattering of shards.
No fruit bowl or basket of laundry.
No framed photo of the father—young,
bare-chested, smiling an easy Thai smile.

*What did you do?* is all you can muster.
She offers a look into the wind tunnel
of her eyes. I start over, she says
looking down at her hands as they dance
out a story. For a moment, it takes her
away. Then she says it again: *I start over.*

# Heart Sutra

My heart is made of sumac twigs
and chicken wire, which, I can say
from experience, is not very good
at keeping in the chickens.
Every morning they're loose somehow,
clucking at my heels as I come
down the steps, swinging the bucket.
Sometimes one saunters off, but mostly
they follow me back to the coop, content
to warble in their clouds of feather dust,
all those unhatched eggs in the straw.

Some days I open the gate, urge them
to abandon the known, wave
my pale thin wings toward the world:
      *Go forth*, I tell them. *Fly!*

But they're not inclined toward flight—
Big Mama Blue Moon, Granny Apple
Red, all the scraggly, three-toed crones.
They stick to the yard where they pace
in circles and coo. They sidle up sideways
on wiry feet, cock their heads and offer
a tiny, one-eyed view of the firmament.
It's messy, this barnyard of the heart;
our only hope is to scatter grain and water,
let the squawking blow through us,
let the barn gate bang in the wind.

# Palmistry

What almost no one knows
about reading palms
is that people tell you things—
with their hands open. In yours.

The celibate talks about the irksome parade
of loose and lovely women. The wide-eyed
girl says she's heard the word fame,
but can't remember what it means.

When you point out the artist's line, the old
painter pulls his palm back. *Maybe,* he'll say.
*If I'd have put more heart in. But I dabbled
in mediocrity, and there's nothing sadder*

*than that.* Then he'll exhale so fully,
he'll scatter the stars on the gypsy cloth;
the ghosts that have gathered will look down
at the folded helplessness in their laps.

The frozen congregation will hold
its collective breath, till
the crestfallen lets his hand drift back,
lets it rest again in yours.

# Homeopathy

Have a sip of what ails you,
drink from the cup of what
you would banish. Open the door
for your qualms and ghouls—
welcome the shadow of their shadows.

Line up the tinctures in smoked glass jars:
distillation of toothache, insomnia, fear . . .
Bring the kettle to a boil; let your troubles thicken.

Listen, meanwhile, as the poles rev up.
Prepare for their Great Shift.
300 mile-an-hour winds, they say.
Nothing vertical left
to stand: Lie down.

Drop the remedies under the tongue:
chilies for argument, ice-chips
for nights you turned away, rust of nail
for believing too hard, eraser shreds
for the truth you denied. To this add

eye of salamander—for persistence
of the downward gaze, our
over-zealous grip
on the ground.

Open your hands now.

For dear life.

Here come the winds.

# Dissolve

*"You only have to let the soft animal of your body*
*love what it loves."*

—Mary Oliver

But everything the body loves is so vaporous—
a mandala of colored sand that the monks
run to joyously—giggling, dancing, swinging
their brooms. It's as if something beyond the body
loves everything more than we possibly can
and so keeps taking it back into itself,
turning it into pixels, beaming it up.

Just before she collapsed on the piano
that's what my friend P said she saw—the world
in all its pixels, a rotunda of tiny lights.
Haven't you noticed it yourself sometimes,
felt what's in your hand start to crumble?
The curtains ruffle up and there it is: matter's love
of dissolve, of returning to shimmer.

# Astronomy at the Alzheimer's Clinic

We are talking about stars. Mildred
just told us she couldn't remember
a time when she'd seen them, and I think
maybe the fog that lumbers through
this valley really did swallow the firmament
every night. But suddenly a time rushes back
when indeed the skies opened and there,
like a thief's lining of watches, they were.
*I saw stars!* She cries, a tiny galaxy
spinning at the corner of one eye.

This stops Bea who's been
pacing the outskirts of the circle.
She can see her family lying flat
on the asphalt. It's the fifties, and
*You couldn't begin to count 'em all,*
*the way kids kept poppin' out of us.*
And there they are, crunched together
in a hush on the blacktop, drinking the milky
spill over Ohio's cicada-filled cornrows.

And now we turn to John, digging his way
through a dream. He waits to be sure
we won't give up on him before he lifts
his head, makes the climb to say, *Yes . . .*
*Yes . . . I saw stars. Right there in Petaluma.*
*So bright,* he tells us, *you couldn't*
*do anything about 'em.*

He's given us our last line. I step aside
from the whiteboard to read our poem,
and as an epilogue, Szymborska's,
with a line that stops me as I read:
*We've inherited hope—the gift
of forgetting.* And I wonder what fills
my new friends as they nod their heads,
their star-lit faces round-eyed and rapt.

# Film Noir

*ala Hubble*

You've come late                    and it's difficult
to find your place — none        of what you
      took for empty seats         are.     They're filled
         with men      in black slickers.


      Central Casting      is enamored with giants
                  and dwarves,
bright faces                  blushing in the lens.     The director
      prefers shadow to subject.      The writer is
            anachronistic—
   by the time
      he's pulled his stories            up,
            the plot's already unwound,
         the actors      long ago      flickered out.


The projectionist,                  old as the hills
                  herself,
sits and watches from
            her little room behind
                  your eyes,
      a room she shares with            black holes, those


notoriously      messy eaters      flinging
      out stars      like popcorn
            under the unlit      dome.


50

# Smoke

I floated through the night half-awake,
a water skater on the dark skin of sleep.
Head in those ethers where crows shoot
dice and houses lift off like rockets.

In the morning I didn't swim up
to the alarm, but flapped down.
The world so unfamiliar, coming to it
this way: blurred gray-tones, smell
of charcoal, as if it had been hastily
sketched in. And later, in the car,

with the radio. All the staticky talk
of the shootings. *Resident alien* they
called him, to which I said out loud,
*who isn't?* In the end, he turned the gun
on himself, the usual close to the story.
You can imagine it, can't you? Shooting
and shooting

until the world stops breathing,
lies bleeding at your feet. Your rage
exhausted, up in smoke. Empty now,
love finds its way in. Everything slides
into place. You see that the girl
in embroidered jeans and mary janes

wears your face; the boy in a ball
on the floor, your hands. It's you who's

spread all over and dying. What fills
the gunman next, we can't say—what
leaden mix of remorse and grief—
so ignorant we are in the ways of love.
But this isn't the poem I started out
to write. I wanted to say how

the children looked when I got
to the schoolyard. How they ran
across the grass, joy twirling
and bobbling their bodies;
their windblown hair
catching fire in the morning light.

# Drawing the Line

*Everybody's gotta have a place for their stuff.*
*That's what life is all about . . .*

—George Carlin

Up to our necks and the floodline
rising, it finally occurs to us we've gone
too far with these opposable thumbs,
this insatiable hankering for things.
*How do you put this spell in reverse?*
We need to go back, retrace our
steps, draw the line. But where?
Certainly not before the wheel or loom.
Not before the fountain pen or sewing needle,
the hammock, the porch light, the hand-blown
pitcher. Not before the guitar.
Surely we would not want to go back before
windows with screens or cameras with zoom
lenses. Not before prisms or wind chimes,
roller skates or Frisbees. Not before fireworks,
or at least not sparklers. Surely we'd want
to keep music boxes and cloth-bound books,
ceramic bowls and flannel pajamas. And what
about the microscope and penicillin, laser surgery
and the Hubble Telescope? Yes, maybe we could
live without memory-foam pillows and hot
showers, but we'd be an achier, grumpier lot.
So when it's time to load up the ark—this time
with only *one* of everything—I hope you'll forgive

me for bringing the fuzzy wool hat Bibi crocheted for me
*and* the floppy-brimmed one Dennis bought me at the beach;
the set of six bangle bracelets from one daughter, the hand-
beaded one from the other. Forgive me if I bring two shoeboxes
of photographs, two reams of watercolor paper and at least five
brushes of varying sizes and shapes. And my silver cruiser bicycle
with its two big saddlebags. I mean how much room could a comfort-bike
with great shocks and two quilted green, wide-mouthed saddlebags take?

# Instead

Instead of certainty, magpies
Instead of sunlight on the water, tears
Instead of hurry, a speckled egg
Instead of worry, the autumn lake
Instead of bitterness, soup
Instead of money, rain
Instead of hope, trust
Instead of blame, laundry on a line—

      a jitterbug of pant legs and sleeves

# Moonscaped Guardian of the World

After months of pleading she gave
in to her seven-year-old son.
Took him for a buzz cut.

Down came the waving wheat stalks,
up rose the vulnerable moonscape
of his head. If he had his druthers,

he'd be shaved to the scalp, she says,
a regular second-grade skin-head.
Don't worry, I say. I've heard of certain

African tribes, where as soon as a baby
arrives, his head and all its hairs are his.
Children stumble through the village,

locks in their eyes. No one will interfere
until the child mentions it. Asks maybe,
What happened to that world of light?

In the Australian bush deliberations
over children's names are short—
parents just give working titles.

Once the kids get the hang of handles—
gecko and wallaby, ginkgo and koala—
their souls are theirs for the naming:

Lorikeet Princess, Termite King, Master
of the Stick Dance and Goatskin Drum.
Moonscaped Guardian of the World.

# Radiance Among Us
### *a suite of troubles*

*All angels are terrible.*

—Rainer Maria Rilke

## *Morning*

unsettles: the first pale moths
of light flicker on the walls.
And the toddler, up
before everyone else in your skull,
thrumps away in the stairwells.

One thing seeps into the next—
scrub oak/crow/coffee steam/
cloud. All in cahoots against
the certainties of noon.

And no one is dead yet.
The departed who sailed
backward through your dream
are just putting on their raincoats
and galoshes, poking through
the umbrella stand. If you turn
now, you'll see them, arm
in arm, heading out into the rain.

## Summer

All day the sunflowers
turn in perfect unison—
a citizenry of haloed faces,
lifted to their blazing god.

We while away
under the same sun, our shadows
lengthen in time with theirs,
are tossed by the same warm
winds. But our eyes
aren't made for fire.

## Flowers

How easily
they pull us in—
the grief-stricken
and the bees.
Fickle flamencos
in ruffled skirts,
their breath
a perfumed sigh.

They'll abandon us,
you know, for the first
zoot-suited gigolo of light.

And they'll drop
him too,
eventually,

for the simpler joys
of fade and scatter.
In the end
we'll be left
with nothing
but the dark seed
they've tucked
in their pockets—
sheathed in nectar
so thick and sweet,
it drives
the scrub jays wild.

## Creatures

Opossums peer down
from the branches—
a congress of whiskered
noses pointed our way.
They'll blink and blink,
but they won't come down.

Finally, dusk gathers, spins
us to a whisper, convinces us
to give up the ghost.
But on the drive home, already
we'll miss them—their nesting
and gnawing, the perfect little
Chinese puzzle they make
when they fold up together
and sleep.

## Stars

The trouble with stars
is all the dust
and noise.

It seems
they never stop
talking, but all we get
are sizzle and shine.

And once in a while
one calling our name.

This haunting, and the constant
shower of ash that sifts down
through the moth-eaten sky.

Whoever lives up there
must be beating the rugs.

## Love

likes you cracked and crumbling—
with the paint peeled off.

Your overcoat thread-bare,
back forty up in smoke—

brush fires at large
in the wind-carved gorge.

Love wants you breathless, dark
and iridescent as coal. Simple

as rain. Useless, stretched-out,
spreadable like lamplight on snow.

Love wants to pour you
from this world to the next.

## Your Childhood

She's going to outlive you—
crouched in the reeds,
blackberry fingers, scabby knees.

Lost to you,
even though her scent lingers
at the back of your tongue.

She's wild enough to stay
hidden, sad as anything
to watch the flurry

of your grown-up
rice-paper, wheat-pasted wits.

## Moon

No matter how many times
you climb the ladder and bring
her down, she floats back up—

gypsy moth, broom-swept queen,
empress of the land of loons.

Oblivious to lock and gate,
she worms her way in.
Not where you wanted her.
The missing silver
winds up in your hair.

# THREE

Yet how often
the heart
that set out for Peru
arrives in China,

—Jane Hirshfield, *China*

# Morning Raga

Birds still folded
in their branches,
trucks asleep
in their blacktopped yards.

Storm's unwound.

The music steps toward us
through the dark:
tabla, ektara, bamboo flute.

The strings and skins,
the woodwinds know,
in their blind love,
where to dig the well.

# Keeping It Simple

The morning is cold,
the teacup warm. The sun,
though far away,
gives all she has.
A gray-bellied dove
teeters for balance
on the feeder.
A shudder of shadow
moves over the questions
and hills. Later I'll
write about the window.
And wind—the one
that's always moving
things around. Today,
though, I'm going to
keep it simple: a cat
at the door and tea
going cool in the cup.
The sound of a pencil
muttering in tongues,
though it might just be slang
nobody in these parts
understands.

# Frogs, Deer, Kitchen Window

*There isn't any way to keep
the kitchen window from tapping.*

—William Stafford

Or the deer from eating the roses,
or the frogs from swallowing the moon.
Or the banjo from midnight,
the sailor from his grief.

There's no way to stop
the whelm of flood tide,
the relentless coloring and
draining of the sky.

Last night we found a wooden bench
on the cliff, its weathered legs longer
than our own. We sat and swung
our feet out over the sea, the body
of your boyhood alive again,
throwing itself into the widening
gap between the worlds.

The trouble with everything
is the way it's so bent on turning:
rose to deer, frog to moon.
Our bodies to the starry cyclone's
empty eye.

# Man without a Wishbone

Blessed with jawbone, elbow and knee,
a tongue for tasting, fingers to touch.
The lantern of his heart swings from its ribcage.
The miracle of his lungs.
But no wishbone bridges the yes and no of him.

When the genie rises from the lamp
he never knows what to ask for.
When the meteors storm an August night,
everyone matching hope to flicker,
he stands dumbstruck.

One day he froze at a fountain,
unable to toss his bright coin.
The marble mermaid took him in, gave
him watch over the cherubs. All spring
the children climbed the ladder

of his spine, pigeons made nests
in his arms, flowers grew from the curled
rim of his hat. These days I wonder
about the strange gift of wantlessness.

However we come by it: birth
or a long life of being nibbled away
by paper moths and summer rain.

# The Year the Gypsy Stayed

The chorus of ankle bell
and cattle hoof, clack and clatter
of wooden wheels dissolved like sugar
in her mouth. And silence grew up
around her, tangled as nettles.
By December she was dizzy
with comings and goings—swallow
and goose, chrysanthemum and poppy,
the rise and fall of honor and shame.
She'd developed a taste for the sweet
dense roots that ripen in the dark.

But the wing-bones ached beneath her skin,
and she couldn't quite parse kettle-sigh
from shaman-breath, dog-moan from
tent-lines in the wind. And she couldn't shake
her love for making fires—cracking
the kindling, lighting the match. Every night
the flames leapt to tell the same story:
Caravanserai burning, herds moving on,
all the gypsies huddled beneath their star-map.
The horizon always at its perfect distance—
unreachable as a lover's dream.

# For the Vagabond

A pear tree, a hopscotch board,
a park bench with pigeons
to keep the old man warm.

And for the rest—a story
with thieves, in three voices:
bumblebee, oboe, wind-sob
in the eaves.

# On the Way Home

It struck me I'd forgotten to thank the sheep for my sweater
and socks, for the boiled wool tops of my clogs.
The trees for the cork and rubber of my soles,
the curved sanded grip of my umbrella.

I'd forgotten to thank the cows for their leather, the geese
for their down. The cotton field and its pickers;
weavers and dyers and basters of the seam.

It went on like this till my house was thronged with the unsung:
soap-makers and potters; carpenters and smiths.
The guys from the paper mill chatted up the farm girls
who churn the butter and grind the wheat.

And finally the troupe that just flits through—
guitar riffs and radio waves, the relentless chitter
of squirrels. And the crows, of course, who
mostly stand around like holes in snow—

those beady-eyed cousins who ring us in darkness,
so devoted to ruckus, so ready to forgive.

# Sundown

I hold no sway in the precinct on the sill.
I'm the gardener—arrange the pots, water
the hopeful, haul off the dead. The Buddha
reclining in the shade of the violets

was my idea. Once a day a streak of color
steals in through the windows crazed
with frost. The Buddha, the leaves, all of it
gets touched as the sun slips down.

It's an illusion, of course. The sun doesn't
go down, it's our own turning away.
Still, I think of this hour as mine, what
in India we called *cowdust time*—when
the beasts sauntered back, kicking up
dust, the world briefly foolish with gold.

Here it comes now, its shadows
of snow on snow. A little light
for the jade-juice drinkers
who rock beneath the jade tree
and the potted paperwhites
who flush behind paperwhite masks.

The Buddha gives in, lets go a sigh,
like the travelers I once saw around the shrine
at *Wat Poh:* pilgrims all over the grass,
making pillows of the scattered stones.

# Miracles

Miracles were better back then.
Italy's St. Emidio, Shepherdess Solange
of Gaul, both of whom strolled around
with their heads in their hands.
Or St. Denis, who famously carried
his severed head from Montmartre,
north to the graveyard where he wanted
his grave, delivering a sermon all the way.
He told his people not to be afraid. He'd seen
the truth: There's more to life than a head
on the shoulders. Oh brothers and sisters,
loosen those frantic grips on your wits.

Well, that might not be exactly what he said,
but it seems like a message that could seep up
once your head's gone and you stumble
indiscriminately into forgiveness.
And that's what I thought I heard today,
coming in on the free-floating sadness
that poured through the windows. And I know
it doesn't seem like much—my walk
to Barry Park this morning, October's gold
breaking over me, odd little life in hand—
but for a while, it was enough.

# Magdalene Faces the Tribunal of Quantifiable Evidence and Measurable Outcomes

Yes, it is possible, I suppose, that he
hypnotized us and we only imagined
ourselves in those silent depths—
that he tricked our minds into peace,
our bodies into ease, created the illusion
that we were whole.

And yes, perhaps we merely felt as if
we were loved . . . with abandon . . .
He smelled like rain and his voice
made my bones hum like a thousand dulcimers . . .

Yes, it was probably just an imaginary wind
that brought us to his feet and blew us back
into lives that are now, somehow, on fire.

And I suppose one could make the case
that he faked the whole thing, that he
was just like the rest of us—lost, tiny
as a grain of rice in a bubbling kettle
of stars. He may have only brought laughter
to our days and dancing to our feet, only
made it seem a blessing to be alive.

No, sirs, I have nothing to show.
None of us got rich or made ourselves
a name. But often I find my pillow wet
when I wake in the night and think of him.

# Rise

It's not that I'm anti-gravity. I like finding things
where I left them as much as anybody—hat
on its hook, avocados in their bowl, foot in its shoe

on the ground. I love when that magnetic force
draws the birds back to their trees—when a swoop
of green parrots, say, drops back into the banyans.

Gravity is one of the three blessings, as all bodies
know when they splash down into their feather beds
and when our high-flung schemes give way to a sigh.

But if it were only the downward pull, we'd wind up
in one big heap—a pile of ice-skates and sauerkraut,
garlic-lilac burnt-rubber smell, old bald men and cigars.

We couldn't pry the laughter from the sobbing,
the garden from the wreck, the downcast queen
from the fisherman, sketch of the loon from the loon.

Which leads to the question: what is it that lifts us all
into our shapes: automobiles and bridges, bamboo and
baby frogs? What nudges us upright in the morning,
starts the humming, stirs in the creamer, raises the cup?

# Moving To Florida

He broke like a wave over breakfast,
saying he wanted to die by the sea.

Not right away, of course,
she's hasty to add. He smiles
and nods, vague eyes adrift.

They'll make their move when the snows
begin to melt. Everything bleeding
and weeping again. Give up the rigmarole

of rudder and rigging, anchor
and sail. Abandon themselves
to the current's whim.

# Our Dimming Stars
## *(a Lament for the Erosion of the Night)*

We've frightened off the stars,
along with so many radiant
mammals of the sea.
But they watch us—
their upright cousins
who move through twilight
as if it were water.

If only we could turn down
the fury of our flames,
maybe they'd paddle back,
lean toward us again,
and blink
those spellbound eyes.

# How I Want to Hear the News

I'd like to be dressed in loose-fitting
clothes. No shoes, though I wouldn't mind
a decent pair of socks—ones that don't
slide down. Still plush in the toes.

And a window that looks out over
trees. Not necessarily in bloom,
but green and breathing. Root balls big
as storm clouds roiling underneath.

I do not want the phone call before
daybreak, cracked Texaco sign turning
in the window. Or the friend at the door
with bug-like complications for eyes.

I'd choose winter, the trees in the
window evergreen. *No,* an inner voice
objects. *Summer! Summer, you fool!*
But I'll take winter, its endless nights

and god-empty days—the sound
of snow disappearing into the sea.
A world without commotion,
except for what thrives in cold.

# Nothing to Declare

The strangeness moves in closer.
A duck drops onto the water.
The wind tosses a curtain
across the way. A face
at the back of the subway
softens in your direction.
The shades roll up inside
your lover's eyes—
luminous stranger briefly there,
fixing a tuna sandwich.

These visits leave their holes
in you. Gaps. Empty stretches
in the traffic noise, as if the thought-
machine shut off. And when
you open your mouth, joy
flies out . . . Joy, of all things.
And that eerie little whistle
you emit now as you pass
through rooms—riddled-through
as you are, like a birdcage.
Gilt worn off, windows ajar.

# Acknowledgments

Grateful acknowledgment is made to the following publications in which some of these poems first appeared:

## *Journals*

*A Cappella Zoo:* "Man without a Wishbone"
*Atlanta Review:* "The Three of Us"
*Barrow Street:* "What the Dark Does"
*Chautauqua Review:* "Disarray"
*Chattahoochee Review:* "Deplaning"
*Comstock Review:* "Noble Thief" and "Christmas Eve at Rite-Aid"
*The Kerf:* "Moonscaped Guardian of the World," "Nocturne," "Two
    Kinds"
*Main Street Rag:* "Heart Sutra"
*Memoir (and):* "Temple of Bees"
*Rattle:* "Electrodomestico," "Mr. James's Marvelous Thing"
*Verbal Seduction:* "Inheritance"

## *Anthologies*

*A Knock at the Door:* "Signs: Kamala Beach"
*Bestiary (A Cappella Zoo "Best of" Commemorative Issue):* "Man without a Wishbone."
*California Poets in the Schools 50th Anniversary Anthology:* "Instead"
*Crossing Lines:* "My Last blind Date
*In the Company of Women:* "grandson, how is this polite little world" (published
    under the title, "Nautica")
*Marin Poetry Center Anthologies, 2008:* "The Year the Gypsy Stayed," "Frogs, Deer,
    Kitchen Window." 2009: "Discipline"; 2010: "Astronomy at the Alzheimer's
Clinic"; 2011: "Drawing the Line"; 2013: "The Hypnotist"; 2014: "Sundown"
*River of Earth and Sky: Poems for the 21st Century:* "Frogs, Deer, Kitchen Window,"
    "Heart Sutra," and "Smoke."